White Stucco Black Wing

White Stucco Black Wing

poems

Karen Kevorkian

Red Hen Press Los Angeles

WHITE STUCCO BLACK WING

Cover image "Wall with Trees" © 1976 Catherine Wagner.
Gift of Graham Nash, m.83.317.75.
Los Angeles County Museum of Art.

Book and cover design by Mark E. Cull.

ISBN 1-888996-78-1
Library of Congress Catalog Card Number: 2003098414

The City of Los Angeles Cultural Affairs Department,
California Arts Council, and
the Los Angeles County Arts Commission
partially support Red Hen Press.

Red Hen Press
www.redhen.org

First Edition

Grateful acknowledgment is made to the editors and staffs of the following magazines in which these poems appeared: *88: A Journal of American Poetry, Third Coast, Rio Grande Review, Runes: A Review of Poetry, Borderlands: Texas Poetry Review,* and *VOLT.* Chapbook publication occurred in a limited letterpress edition made at the Virginia Arts of the Book Center and online at *The Drunken Boat* (http://thedrunkenboat.com).

I am also very grateful to the MacDowell Colony, the Djerassi Foundation, and the Ucross Foundation for time to work.

Special thanks to Kate Gale, Gail Wronsky, and Richard McCann.

Thanks are also owed to willing readers Elisabeth Frost, Judy Juanita, Carlene Laughlin, Tillie Olsen, Lisa Russ Spaar, Dell Upton, and Charles Wilmuth, and to Greg Orr for help early on. And to Nin Wilson, Anna Skinner, Raffi Kevorkian, Ellina Kevorkian, Soseh Kevorkian, David Skinner, Greg Eklund, Desmund Eklund, and Stefan Siegel.

"This Is the World," "Olive Lingering," "Hokum," "Rain Stutters on the Portico," "Lone Star Cement," and "This Membrane Hour This Liminal" are in memory of Olive Sanderson Snipes, 1895 – 2002.

For Dell

Contents

Imagine a city where nothing's forgiven

— Adrienne Rich
"Rusted Legacy"

Wheeze of Steadily Burning

Wheeze of steadily burning fire or a cat swishing through tissue
or a woman in a basement apartment straining from a window
to reach bras and underpants hanging from a line

slack between two buildings to cover them with plastic
this space of no particular use a conjunction

two three-storied E-shaped buildings
rain turning over to itself
the idea of repetition

gusts scraping dangling silver pipes
a charm of sound. Cantonese vowels swaying

down the cul de sac. Toilet flushing. Yesterday
a chicken dying window to the right
awk awk awk this unmistakable dying

El Camino Real

As in
            Maxfield Parrish, though he wasn't
Californian. Still,

that's what it feels like

after dawn, or when the sun
declines, when a shadow's black wing
cuts white stucco, the street for a minute
quiet, then
a child cries, or a
radio speaks
                    the inky fluttering tip of a crow's wing

disappears over the white edge of a roof. Between buildings

palm trees effloresce, wide spray of
green fronds, something processionally
to bear. Ah, Aida.

Maybe. Less
grandly

new trees ringed with metal

staked, what's
to come

Where Filbert Met Kearny

White apartment buildings surged down the hill
then they climbed so bone pale. Did my heart

beat hot or was I
a string of tape unreeling the taught? Heart
in my hat. That fine hat
of gold shaking feathers their whisper
too lately come.

Locked in my three rooms the key rasped *safe.*

Or was it *soft?*

Imagine Your Body

Imagine your body inlaid with mirrors recording
what passes and passes
away. Move quickly

and there is a sound like the shimmer of
a thin sheet of metal like the tinny rumble of
stage thunder.

                    Or think of
cement lawn furniture in the south where broken
ceramics and mirrors are pressed into mineral
a tabletop patchy and fantastic
                                        all that passes
part of this surface yet nothing lingers
                              like cloud shadows
on the ground or an airplane passing. Or a rough
plaster figure into whose chest someone
cuts
a small round window.

Tiny Yellow Mums

Tiny yellow mums in the green plastic
hardware store pot bunch dryly.

Higher than the sex toy trees
a lone bird drifts. Wish again

for a city's fire escape where the
tiny dog etc. and the screaming orange-hair.

In the alley she and the wet gunk
of a street where stores are. That easy hello

those who speak because you've
paid them. A table here. There a
jacket. Flowers and some
cartons of milk. By such things

you know yourself and when you walk
into your rooms that you
close the door and lock it firmly.

lists of observed things
apparently in no order but in
an emotional order

In the Pages You're Turning Tonight

The virgin nods at the pale crouching angel as if wanting
to catch every whisper

her blue kimono thatched in black lines like September's dry grass
along California's coast where under cattleguards
lie the crisp and negligently twisted

peeled off like a glove or silk sweater writhed out of skins of rattlers

and in hills distant the breathless small houses
everyone gone to cities
all that's left

a garden of greens with broad leaves forever gone to seed

and the snake whose hiss is like a cat's

not the tamed silver snake whose tiny head snagged your black slip

the white wall outside snarled with black wire
and more wire snarling sky

hard rain melting the words *we will miss you*
a sign by a green florist's vase left standing on the curb

someone else faded like the virgin leaning forward on her bench

her robe dramatically pale though at this moment
she hasn't vanished

as you feared you would do when living alone
so you stopped
sleeping naked

the woman from the street would press her palms together
bowing for the quarter you let lapse from your hand

terror renders transparence

a silver snake no armor
a black silk skin no camouflage
for questions the virgin not yet pregnant or ravenous asks.

image! rich
Olena

The News

Scientists call the network of branching bubble
universes the "multiverse." It could
continue forever.

— *The New York Times*

Sliding out of the black and white photo
a boy
    head turned aside one hand
covering face
        what does he see

two kerchiefed women
hands held forth like
welcome

mouths little Os of pain

behind them
concrete torrents of wall

It Was a Cold Room

It was a cold room but the light from the round white thing
was bright as all hottest, raging, acetylene sparks
scissoring steel. The woman in the bed lay

burning or thought she did. The woman in the bed

lay in a sweat running cold on her face and her bare
arms under the hot cold of this light shadowing

this pleasant conceit

the someone looking out over all
notions of first
combining
wind smashing
planets in a dance

pull and tug and explosions
that fiery hurtling
into dark
scar of impact.

Her Clothes Weren't Quite Right for the New Town

The afternoon is pleasant. Why shouldn't it be?
It is wearing grace and pain; it is dressed like a woman.
— César Vallejo, "Down to the Dregs"

Trees dazzling the roof,
Rain went to her closet and tried to find
something to wear. Something brilliant, unequivocal,
liquid thunder.
                    Too much black,
                    Rain said. At least
give me
sequins.
          What
          followed:

                    red clay buoying water
water slithering
                    exuberant
gutters
          little Versailles.
                                        Oh wind me
you bedsheet sky.

                    Cocoon? The task of opening
all the boxes on the floor. All the sleeves inside

flowing out onto

It's Muggy Here

The green sheen of rain wore down her mineral

her flint sluiced

she'd come so far for this
one thing and it was just

another thing

a daily swim through the blank
sun of afternoon

the terrible green

The Green Canal

You'll always end up in this city.
— C. P. Cavafy, "The City"

This won't hurt this won't and again if you do it like this.

This won't hurt if you do it like this and again like this. Every moment

you're running out of. And you don't depend on. It doesn't work like

This. Breathing in and out with your steps. Yellow light on glassy brown
green canal water that
silklike

slips by. Benediction
of pavement. Cold on cheeks. Legs pump. Writing in the cold

fluorescent room and outside morning cars flower then fade

Today working from five in the morning no break. Later when I walked out rain and cold yielding to balmy and gorgeous light. I sat at a café by the canal. Writing you this. A state of mild well being from white wine and sun. You moved to change your life. This said simply as a child. I woke in the night you were gone. I plunged through dark. Of course we did not know in New York our friend, the poet, also gone, in that swift way death can have so non metaphorical.

Then the caramelized leeks
evergreen chard white
turbot. The sum
ever more than the parts. The café was empty
the host with his big smile. A woman inclined above white bowls
droning a flat nasal song. A man cupping his ear. In each bowl
a red claw waved. In the air tufted seed
moths in gelid light
unresistant. She

the leek-eater leaning back into the wall the white cloth
destroyed now
a white plate smeared brown
looking through the door
the canal running so smoothly
and it seemed with a little shove she would topple

Each end panel of the triptych shows a half room that closed conceals
the crowned queen of heaven
          and in the corner the angel
crouching with parroty wings bearing the message of a changed life.

                                        If the end panels were closed
as they never are
they would meet to make a whole, a room before the virgin
before the angel. In its windows
far towers of another mythical city
where pigeons struggle and preen
their feathers released bits of smoke

Differently
What would you have done
differently
asked while you were doing
what? Complaining in that
mewling way of an elderly
yellow cat. Ow. Ow. And then
more Ow.

In your body the heavy agitation you lay
on the white sheet stretched taut on the old mattress.
Oh
fluttering. Oh ferment. Oh loss.

An umbrella's black circle imposes double dark
for those who taste pain blooming in the body like a hot rose. The desire
to possess the city is like drink, which is wanting to lose herself. Like sex.
Try not to drown
walking beside water brilliant with music and light.
A surface that does not beg penetration
but only to return that which is passing
and isn't that what sex is for her now?
To lose herself alongside the canal's still water may restore her soul
here in the valley
under a street's downward pouring light those
cones of gold
breath of car exhaust and perfume

tall chestnuts' creamy flower mounds like wax from candles
burned the whole night. Flowers for a bride's wreath
and kid gloves in a glass case
yellowed fingers shriveled
could only fit a child.
A leaning forward in her gait she rakes
her uncombed hair its strands ecstatic
heavy silver on the wrists
blue veins on backs of hands
shoulders drawn together narrow the body down. Drowning
what is it she needs?
more water more flood deeper

yielding

Hurrying along opaque green water
its rising faint odor of rot
exhalation of foundations sunk into canals
a green smell
clay brick and mold
death charged
secrets a house keeps
things elude her
always about to grasp what could have been and never quite was.

A dog floating by the shore
slick hair glistening like a rat's
among plastic sacks bobbing like lungs smoothly ballooned. This is what
she remembers
the erasure of cities
sunlight smearing
she wants it

down to the dense, preoccupied,
skeptical green world, that does not know us

— Denise Levertov
"Knowing the Unknown"

Escuela and Rengstorff

Escuela and Rengstorff run into California Street then through to
El Camino Real *where Lieutenant Colonel Juan Bautista de Anza*
and party crossed this area in March 1776 en route to select sites for the
presidio and mission of San Francisco

and where, Fray Pedro Font wrote that same month

they came upon an Indian carrying grass. Seeing them, he
manifested the greatest possible fright,
holding out his bunch of grass
as if by this present he hoped to save his life.

The air swarming with ospreys, eagles, condors. And on the ground
antelopes, grizzlies, elk, and wolves roaming. Rabbits you could
catch with your hand. Great runs
of salmon and steelhead. Numberless

seals and whales. Ten thousand
Ohlone.
To cross the road you press the button on the pole
stop cars. The way people will
stop, turn,

help a blind woman or man, flash of dark

hands held out, feeling, something to
shrug away from

Loose Sweets

Put on the pale green quilted puffy
jacket about the same green as the dogwood's lower leaves

leaves not yet red
even though red berries litter grass

like Red Hearts spilled and melting.
A night of

chocolate in tiny bars. Latex
corpse masks. Flashlights
twiddling trees.

At the end of the street beneath the lamp
a scalded drive.

Red leaves pave

warm warm
caution.

To Look at the Thing

To look at the thing and in the looking
become.
          It's so

dark here. And
quiet. Though the thumping

is only you shifting your
chair.

This Is the World

The white sky the black
embroidery of leaves. Song
raucous. Coarse
hue. All the small birds
safe in the trees. Liquidity
of skin. Burnish
it. This is not

pastoral. These days the
bright lights swiftly followed
by dark. Don't forget
pain. Why should she crack
the bowl of her bones? Why
should the dying be hard?

Olive Lingering

The sun beat down she hid in the house
          Olive
is ready to pass
                    watching the land that so
flatly spreads
                    We
want her to and do not
want it
                    the low tract houses the green lawn its
                    knifeblade sprout
heat shivering mesquite
          Everybody
waits for it
                    tall cottonwoods that in spring
fizz across lawns
fluff shoring at the curb’s edge
                    Nobody
wants it
                    at dusk
the sprinklers tolling

Hokum

will continue to fight the myth . . . of the global
Islamic revolutionary in the vanguard of holy war
against the West . . . what deadly hokum. . . .
— *The New York Times*

Sirens climb the scale
seamlessly glissand then a
languid decline. She is
looking down now. Heaven.
That choppy sea

car surge toward noon. American flags

clip-on wands. Cold noodle freeway
sprawl. Mi Tierra. Acrylic
Nails. Churches big enough

for 757s. Lots carved from johnson grass,
sunflower, mesquite. Train's velvet call.

Her body
transparent now
flying up. She must be up
if she looks down. The straightened

body. No more kinks. Chiffon dress
smoothed blue. Lipstick

slash. Sleep nested in the quilted

polyester. Cymbidium
just so in clasped hands. Don't she

look beautiful? Oh
there. There.

Rain Stutters on the Portico

In gullies

gray mad surges. Through highway lakes the cars fan plumes
symmetrical. The river insanely fleeing
green electric banks. Invisible gusts loft cattle egrets, stiff
spindle legged. Under thrumming canvas rain

herds us. The mud is yellow,
wild and slick. Wet matted grass of
indecorous
green. Five solemn

grandsons fold their hands. Beside still waters he
leads me. In the valley
of the shadow
                    surely
all is running over now. Leave her to

the acid grass
that springs from earth's
gold ooze. Those bones drying

coral porous.

Lone Star Cement

Dogs bark. Tree frogs
chip away at night. The old plant lit up

like New York. Black starlings' wild cries
from low trees in silhouette

on Nacogdoches opposite new Walgreens'
neon beaconing
dark. Out El Sendero
headlight bleached sunflowers

crazily nod. Car
in the garage. Mad wing
flutter in the laurel. Pavement's
knotted pods and *tesoro*

hard red beans. Snails marathon
up the siding

pulpy wands dowsing skyward their

calling.

This Membrane Hour
This Liminal

Through the hour of dog bark
lace curtain shadow
watery imprisoning
the businesslike cars surge

hour of persistent
water threading pipes

a closet in another room
a ticking along
a metal bar

Every morning bones insistently tell another day

(Oh she was
ready and I wasn't
the only one she)
          Dawn creaks
                              Mozart
on the radio twitter of
keys the occasional
tree frog stipple

not evening's blunt
cicada drone the swell the
hum the subside

Outside's Only

Here the curtain.
The leaves lull they are always
falling budding

twist. Here the red brick
silence that houses are so good at.

The walling out. Because outside's only

bud float fall.

Raw Video Footage

1
Above coarse corn stubble in a red dirt field
like the short body hair of a strawberry blonde

above the dull pond with its one or two
grimy white ducks gliding

the rumbling of planes ignored by still skeletal trees
new leaves like small jade tiles from
an unearthed antique shroud

hiss of yellow jonquils on the ground
pale skin
with barely more intense freckles
that constellate.

she turns stiffly
resigning herself to some blow that eventually
will fall
keeping her face pressed to the white sheet,
the comfort of rough material
on which someone hastily outlined wreathes
in thick cotton thread
a story hinted at
unread

the sky white, too, like
milkglass dishes taken from a house

another sleight of hand
rearrangement. Her pale skin

even paler oh blue white just the color
of winter soaked sand on the island nearby, where ponies run free
delicious that shore all the calm great blues
sentinel in the ditch.

2

                                                          An expressionless woman
squatting in a concrete block room

                                                          the way light falls much isn't left
                                                          of the roof. One after the other
the woman holds plates under water dripping from a tap. Slowly,
almost languorously, she rubs. The camera

travels the wall, passing the window
with its holes that look as if fist-shaped rocks
exactly made them.
                                                          In a corner sits a boy,
hands on knees. Maybe four or five. He never looks away from
the woman in her disregard of the room
                                                          of him
the camera telling it.

Another Brilliant Day

The point was
it wasn't like being anywhere. And after the salty

chips and a green sauced enchilada and one or two
bottles of dark Mexican beer it was back into the car
to drive out into the teasingly warm

night. On the radio whatever it was

singing so that the dark itself was no longer
compromised.

My mind stays nowhere
for more than a second. It's always
been like that but now
its resting time seems
nonexistent. All the time

I feel sad. As in the aftermath

of death. This

I mask.

By six the sun is
bright. In fact at five forty seven
                                        the sky all easter egg
blue and pink. Light clutches
the rims of each of this window's
four panes of glass

Electronic sensate
I've become.

trees exploding

white flowers. Pear trees someone said. The light that all winter
blued through the window shows green. Not just

any blue, any green.

Let yourself
                                        go down into

like a cave where men wait
heads in hands for shelling

to stop. Darker
at the end, at the mouth,

the brightness, fire
                                        go down
into

let yourself
down into the slosh so like the death

of any body of water
brine shrimp
                                        exoskeletons
bunching at the shore

Civilian body count 227
minimum 307
maximum
                                        only the first week.

Another brilliant cold day. Someone cutting
grass. The grass so long that bunches of the long blades
lie all the same way like
                                                shocks of hair.
                        That
                        watermelon smell

razor sharp and green.

Children who look
like they are sleeping when loaded into
the back of a truck, sun

slashing its walls

gentle fly buzz, fingers of their small hands

folded inward on their palms, as though some secret
still tightly held, something they will now

never let go of

What gives you
the right

Where are you
from

In the street now

cars slowing
horns angrily

It was just a place,
that café, somewhere
to be, here

in the Land of White
Noise. Everywhere
a lawn being mowed. Women wearing

tiny American flags of

cubic zirconia. Where in spring

flowered trees lean this way

then another

Warm March wind shakes the glass of this room. Not
harshly. One crow calls. Black thin limbs of small trees

elliptically red budded. Taller trees showing
spring's small green fists.

Does the body move differently
when you walk to the curb in the morning

bend down? And inside the new house how you
spread the pages
the faint crinkle

familiar to your smoothing palm. How you lift

the cup of dark coffee. The tone in which you speak to the cat.

No.
No.

Spread the pages. Who is
crying today? Mother

lost a son. Father lost
three daughters. Child lost
both arms. City lost
fifty
                    from the poorest part, the market.

These scenes are graphic and may contain content
offensive to some. The bodies

                    drawn from their trays in the cabinets.
A child who seems to be dressed

in red. Helplessly
weeping, a big-nosed man
covers his eyes with one hand. A voice says quietly

Mohammed, Mohammed. Then the hospital

where from a boy's body wrapped in white gauze

a plastic tube trails.
                    You see it all.
                    The man raising

the boy's shirt to show us. The boy's hands as he pushes it down.

Aftermath

The vocal-seeming torment
of huge blackbrown boneless-seeming

bodies. Everything is

like. It drifts

uphill and, nearer, a dog
claims its portion of the day. Cars
rustle, hum, the

ordinary life. The dog (from the sound,
medium-sized) gives voice awkwardly. Downhill
the sea lions close eyes and take
deep breaths. How can they sleep? A few feet away

people lean intensely
against wooden rails. Each sleeping pile's
looming bull
                    triumphantly sings. Then

with a blade's grace, one slips into
salty green.

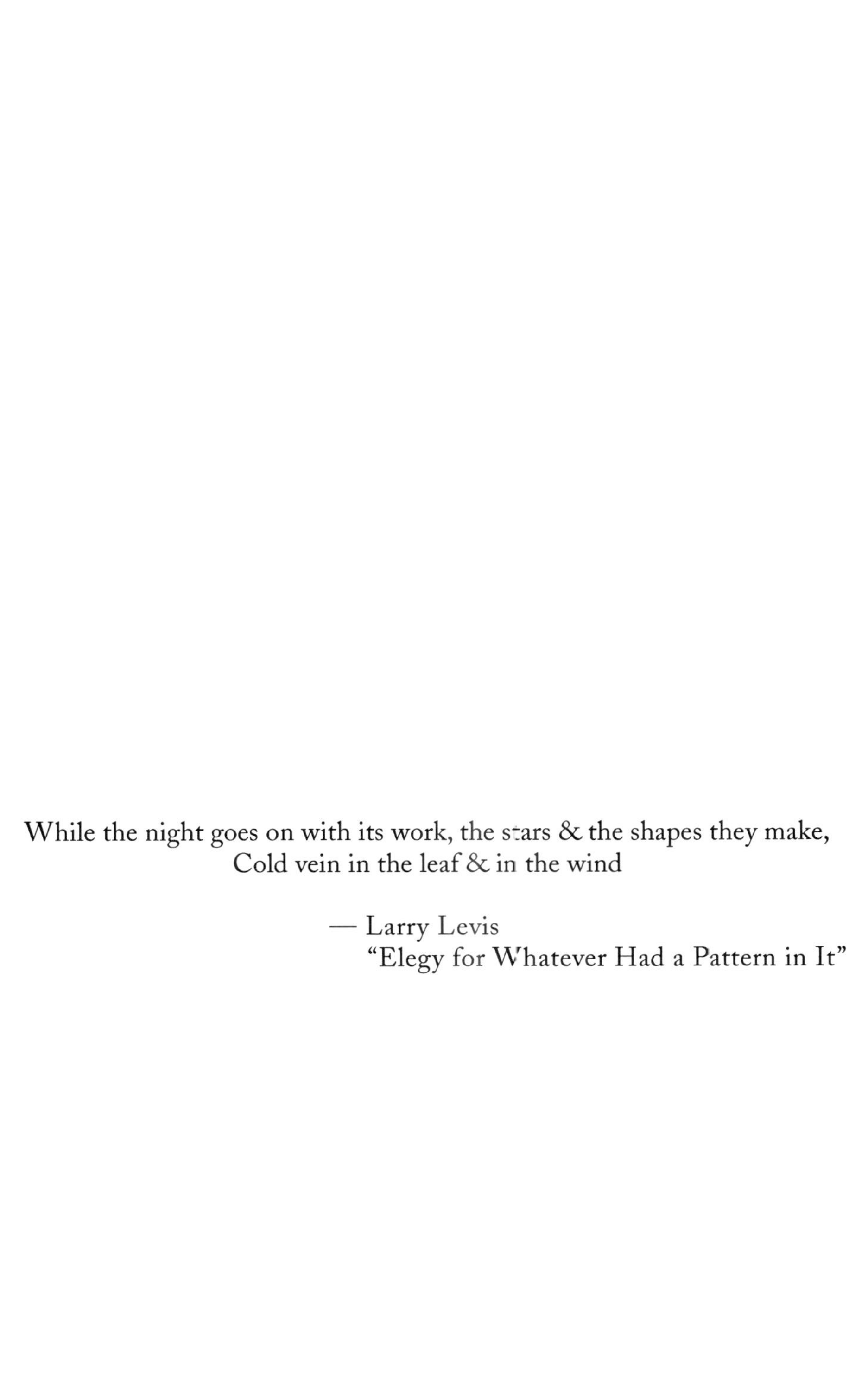

While the night goes on with its work, the stars & the shapes they make,
Cold vein in the leaf & in the wind

— Larry Levis
"Elegy for Whatever Had a Pattern in It"

The Red Dream

Incessant tapping

a woodpecker and overhead
big machinery of fire

Essentially a boys' club where women have no place
oh the military does what it wants

Turkey buzzard in the tulip poplar
sick glistening of its gray wings

red hood
soft whistle

She dreamed a red cross marking ground
so the plane could
find her *(had she shown him*

too much affection?)

Turkey buzzard in the tree top

gunmetal cloak wisping
gnarled rigid red hood
this was not
Disney

all around gray limbs and brick houses
red as tomato soup in a child's white
bowl
the child leaning into its breath

Finally No Evidence

A latex glove in the dirty snow. Plastic quart-size coke classic
half buried. Shreds caught in baretwigged limbs. She falls
on ice. A young man

no thanks. I'm fine. Does he think

her forced smile

how old? When she looks in the mirror her lipstick

mouth blurs. On chapped lips color wantonly
traveling the fine creases. Roughly she
rubs her mouth. Roughly
again. Finally no evidence
of silly desire.

What Kind of Life

What kind of life is this
this ripe this
smooth this unhurrying
                                        ascent and descent

quiet soles slapping shining wood floors
first to go up then
                                        to come down. The faint

dog bark. The faint hammer's
lift and strike.

Lunch

Soft rolls with thin ham

butter without salt. The butter cookie called Little Scholar
with gleaming chocolate

waxlike impression of an antique boy
caught running.

In the Dark Sky

Pillows of snow creeping toward
light. Houses show themselves only by windows,

light they conceal.

High and deep
in the dark sky a sliver

radiant moon. Behind one window
a woman studying her hands.

Soon

The wind's harder breathing
stuttering the window frame. A limited
war. Its limited
deaths.
    Soon

a few months the leaves again
budding. All that
murderous flourishing.

Kisses

See how the trees hold still beneath
their fluffy burden. See how the round holly bush
warms the circle of uncoated ground. See
how the dead vines tangle. Still hoping
for sloppy white kisses on dark bark.

I am not falling no
                    I am still as bone.
Bleached and my black rot concealed.
A winter desert littered with the unburied everywhere

spiky pale extrusions
                    all this covering uncovering
patient as dogs the quiet yawp of falling.
If were kept visible all yr cold kisses
if they stayed one on the other

exoskeletal collection
pale cicada husks
green beetle carapace

                    I felt it so why should it not show?

White Hand Like a Shark Fin

White hand like a shark fin
wave and dip in the window
snow stuttering over

the still car
engine
burbling down

now

the passenger door opening
a woman moving in a way abrupt and not caring

swinging at the windshield snow
light and loose as fragrance

Once I Was in Wyoming

Once I was in Wyoming
Wind at night
tiny toenails of mice in the walls
liquid graffiti

so afraid of
stepping on one
or where they had been

always wearing shoes
even after a bath

unthinkable to touch

at dusk looking out the windows
at the not-too-distant
brown ground

undulant with
small brown rabbits

and in the daylight fear of snakes.
I would sit outside but always
alert-to
no no not my feet in the air
but almost.

Tell me this.
Why are lives so full? I don't mean
spiritually.
I mean like a bucket teeming with
the small jumping green

the wanting-to escape.

At noon I courted heat in the yard.

The small cedar tree
skull of a deer the few branches
of its antlers. I waited

for sun to burn leaves
from the hackberry wispy

papery things. All afternoon I would listen

hard. Wind in the tall grass by the road.
The aluminum gate chained to a cedar post
chattering. You had to yank it

free the chain. But the chain bound the post
so tightly I could barely. Then

more gravelly road but pretty soon
no more tall grass pretty soon

rocky fields. Brilliant feathers dead pheasant

loud announcement in the weeds. No trees
on the horizon

absurd as a shout. In the far away
the Tetons

hawks surging on
drifts of air. I filled my eyes
with what seemed like nothing.

Splitting cedar logs with an axe
the dark metal cleaving the red heart

squirrels writhing in the gray trees
leisurely as smoke
still an occasional red clot
in the withering brown

pain that disheveled
squirrel's nest

leaves bunched at the end of a dead limb

something easy for the wind.

It Was the Idea of Them

That despair verged upon rapture.
— Maurice Blanchot, "The Song of the Sirens"

Invisibly threading their paths through the woods
past the cabin where she sleeps

deer fixed in their forest trails. Star streaks
in time-lapse photography, meaning

it is the mind of the woman sleeping

that turns in the night, the deer establishing
the one point the one place

dreams contradict.
The scent of their passing fixed
odor on a glove
turp from a handful of skinny cones
from the white pine
bright sticky dots on the underside of each wooden petal.

Her first day walking down the dirt road at night
when she still feared

she heard a snorting and whinny. Horses
she said. "A loud *whistling snort* from the woods,
morning or evening, means you have been scented."
                                                                                    She was

hungering and thirsting
for you, not
your creations,
                    but for
yourself,
          O Truth, in whom there is no
variation, no play
of changing shadow.

It is very cold. Sometimes her fingertips inside her black gloves
burn.
    If only it would snow.

Holding out the black hand to receive
its palm's worth of icy
constellations.
        Night

    bracken by the road ignite
pinkly from her light. Face burning
she snuffs the flashlight
leans back as far as she can

looking up.
        It is something like
looking down
        at L.A. on a clear night from a plane
this trying to make out what you see

        La Cienega and Wilshire
picked out by a specialist. Otherwise mere
beauty. Like deer whinnying

unseen behind dead birch leaves tipping tree limbs
and orangely floating.

She lied. Their bodies
not in her dreams. It was the
idea of them
unseeable

but present
lives parallel
nonintersected
skittish prudence
her

eager running
from the house

for what

to see.

And what would seeing change?
The heart speeding at the flashy whitetail? A thing

desired dis-
appearing per-
haps for
ever.

Is this
beauty? She
wants it.

It could be the deer in a painting by
Magritte that white rump
severed by the forest
wall the woman standing

naked in a clearing. Her orangey
fleshtone her blueblack
hair severely
pinned back. Carmine flush those

impassive lips and in a basket
the red blue and green spines
of books.
Only
books?
Something
she wants.

Vocabulary:
That which will not stay
we must have

pray to
make up words for.

Not a being with limbs stretching
far and wide and having a certain size.
(Because then

you'd have that white rump,
disappearing.)

Rather than
present everywhere in its entirety
as spirit is

. . . for unless your ears be present in our deepest places
where shall we go and whither

cry?

Yours is the day
yours the night
Not in vain do harts and hinds seek shelter in these woods

to lie down and ruminate

Perfect me
                    Reveal
those woods to me
                                Give me
what I love for I love
and this love
you have not given me.

A lamp
with cone-shaped shade of white glass
reflected by the window
like another room on the other side

where the day's gestures could be
tried again. On the pane
that separates
her room from the cold
the white cone

oh let me in.

The Actual Life

Gradually your room shadow-limned.
Night then emerges from what there is not. A shift
in the coal-hearted logs like the rustle of dry silk
against smooth skin. And the promise of that marriage

the twitch of sap in the logs. You cannot continue to think

of deer and fire and snow falling from trees. It's not
the actual life. Flames

twist around logs. Little Saint Joans.

Give the fire something to eat.

Tinged with Red Neon Clouds Drift in from the Coast

Here is a story: *A teacher invites students to his house where his wife lies in bed*
in the front room, paralyzed. He never mentions her, and neither do the students
as they step quietly near the body. Following a dusty yellow path

downhill past a water tank and its obsidian surface, a rat-rattling barn,
and all the high pale grass with its dry rasp that may be lizard or wind
yet all walk faster

to the creek where small trees are moss-grimed. Where lichen scabs bark.
Where brown water flows cold over gold stones, where the horsetail, green
anachronism, clouds the opposite bank, where they cross on fat white rocks,
come to the fallen redwood, the base as tall as three, its spindly, mudcaked,
erotic roots. Here is a story: *A dancer watching her performance on film –*
My enemy is time. Here the rain penetrates

and earth gives up hardness, lets go of roots and the tree in its entire being
accedes to the inevitability of dirt, yields to the shudder and fall. So memory
saturates and who survives her story? Though in the end it doesn't matter
whether you are the body celebrated or forgotten, the creek flows
with a sandy accumulation of big trees

casual dust. And all night rain with its hurried thrum and spit. You're
wine-soused, dinner offering some illusion of others except the night
knows better and you wake with a heart full of dread. This isn't poetry

that hustle and sigh. Listening is hard work, the rain with its morse code
antique communicator

the something being told, lying beyond seeming-to-know,
some whisper, promise, release. *Ss-ss* the rain's admonitory,
fingertip tapping.

The wet leaves fluttering with importance. Heave and turn
these messages of night, another coast, and your
irrefutable body.

The How of It

To hear
a piece a composer will
spread the score page by page
on the floor. Draws into herself

color and texture the how of it
moving. This
noiselessly.
Incessant

rain a blind man tapping one hand held out
almost reaching
the how of her

trying to find
a way in the dark

she thumps into wood

oh what is there to do
again the late

quartet dark
brown tea white
grapefruit pith.

Notes

César Vallejo's epigraph for "Her Clothes Weren't Quite Right for the New Town" translated by James Wright.

C. P. Cavafy's epigraph for "The Green Canal" translated by Edmund Keeley and Philip Sherrard.

Lines in "The Green Canal" taken from J. M. Coetzee, *The Master of Petersburg.*

Information in "Escuela and Rengstorff" from Malcolm Margolin, *The Ohlone Way: Indian Life in the San Francisco-Monterey Bay Area.*

Maurice Blanchot's epigraph for "It Was the Idea of Them" translated by Lydia Davis.

Lines in "It Was the Idea of Them" adapted from St. Augustine, *Confessions.*

Karen Kevorkian's poetry and fiction have appeared in numerous magazines, including *Antioch Review, Fiction International, 5 Fingers Review, Hambone, Los Angeles Review, Massachusetts Review, Mississippi Review, Rio Grande Review, River City Review, Third Coast,* and *Virginia Quarterly Review.* She teaches poetry and fiction writing at the University of Virginia.